PRAYERS FOR ALL SEASONS

By the same author

PRAYERS AT BREAKFAST
NOBODY'S PONY *(for Children)*
PONY FOR SALE *(for Children)*

Beryl Bye's

PRAYERS FOR ALL SEASONS

FOR
WOMEN'S MEETINGS

THE LUTTERWORTH PRESS
CAMBRIDGE

The Lutterworth Press
P.O. Box 60
Cambridge CB1 2NT

British Library Cataloguing in Publication Data
Bye, Beryl
    Beryl Bye's prayers for all seasons for women's meetings.
    Prayers for all seasons for women's meetings.
    1. Prayer-books
    Beryl Bye's prayers for all seasons for women's meetings.
    I. Title
    264'.13   BV250

    ISBN 0-7188-1793-1

First published 1971
Reprinted 1973, 1975, 1979, 1987 (with additions), 1990

Printed in Great Britain by
The Guernsey Press Co. Ltd., Guernsey, Channel Islands.

FOREWORD

I WAS invited to write the first edition of this book to meet the needs of those responsible for leading women's meetings.

My aim was to avoid theological language and long and complicated prayers, to bear in mind that not everyone who attends a women's meeting is a wife and/or mother, and to write with specific themes (or speakers) in minds.

I have been encouraged to learn that over the years many leaders have found *Prayers for All Seasons* useful, and in response to a modest demand, I have had pleasure in preparing certain alterations and adding two new prayers. It comes to you with the sincere hope that it will make the important, (but sometimes thankless!) task of leading women's meetings a little easier, whilst emphasising the relevance of the Christian faith to every area of service.

BERYL BYE

FOR PATTI

CONTENTS

Opening   *Reading*

And a scribe came up and said to him,   2 Kings 4: 8–17
"Teacher, I will follow you wherever you go."
And Jesus said to him, "Foxes have holes,
and the birds of the air have nests; but
the Son of man has nowhere to lay his head." (Matt. 8: 19, 20)

Lord of the stable and of the hillsides, we thank You
for the homes that You have given us,
> For a door to shut against the night,
> For a roof and walls to keep out the cold and rain,
> For a fire at which we can warm ourselves,
> For a table at which we can gather to eat and talk.
We pray for those who have no homes and who must live without
> privacy or security.
We pray for those whose only home is a crowded tenement room
> or a rough shelter of planks or corrugated iron.
Lord, in our comfort, remind us of the uncomfortable,
> in our plenty, give us concern for all those in need.   Amen.

Lord, Show us how we can use our homes in Your service,
> Show us a lonely person whom we can invite to a meal,
> Show us a tired person to whom we can give a holiday,
> Show us a shy person who needs mothering,
> Show us a Christian with whom we can share fellowship
that both our doors and our hearts may always be open in love.
                                                        Amen.

Closing

Jesus once gave a man these instructions, "Go home to your friends
and tell them how much the Lord has done for you, and how he has
mercy on you." The man went away and began to proclaim how
much Jesus had done for him and all men marvelled.

  May we too cause people to marvel as we go home and show
what the Lord has done for us.   Amen.

OLD AGE

Opening   *Reading*

It is good to give thanks to the Lord,   Psalm 92: 5–15
to sing praises to thy name, O Most High;
to declare thy steadfast love in the
morning, and thy faithfulness by night. (Psalm 92: 1, 2)

Almighty and Everlasting God,
    We know that all who are granted a full span of life must one day experience the limitations of old age.
    If we are old, Lord, grant us a sweetness of nature that will attract others to us when we are unable to go to them.
    Give us the patience with human shortcomings that comes as a result of experience.
    Show us when to stop talking, so that we can listen instead.
    Help us to bear pain silently.
    And to share our joys and not our complaints,
    So that as we grow in age, we may grow also in grace.   Amen.

O Lord,
    Help us to understand the problems and sorrows that old age can bring and to be ever ready to help and cheer.
    Help us to show interest even when we have heard the same story again and again.
    Reduce the speed at which we walk so that we may keep pace with slower steps.
    Raise our voices so that they may be more easily heard.
    Quicken our reactions so that we may be swift to see when help is needed.
    Help us to be patient with ailing bodies, fussy appetites and querulous tempers, remembering that we shall one day be old and long for others to be patient with us.   Amen.

Closing

Grow in the grace and knowledge of our Lord and Saviour Jesus Christ. To Him be the glory both now and to the day of eternity. Amen.

Opening   *Reading*

A friend loves at all times, and a   Proverbs 27: 1–10
brother is born for adversity. (Proverbs 17: 17)

Heavenly Father, we would thank You today for our friends.
For those who live near to us and for those who are far away.
For those who look after our children, do our errands and visit us
    when we are sick.
For those who listen to our troubles and cheer us up when we are
    depressed.
For those who encourage us in our Christian lives and give us
    confidence to tackle tasks of which we feel incapable.
We thank You for the friends who write to us and the friends who
    phone us up. The friends with whom we have a morning cup
    of coffee, or an afternoon cup of tea. The friends who lend us
    magazines, bring us produce from their gardens, or jars of jam
    and marmalade which they have made. The friends who know
    us best and love us in spite of all our faults and failings, and who
    stand by us at the times we need them most.
Heavenly Father, we would thank You today for our friends. Amen.

Lord, Help us to be the best kind of friend,
    Help us to be loyal and not to talk about people behind their
        backs.
    Help us to be thoughtful—seeing what needs to be done
        without having to be asked.
    Help us to be tactful—never saying or doing things that are
        hurtful.
    Help us to be constant and reliable so that we can always be
        depended upon.
O Everlasting Friend, help us to be the kind of friend whose love
    will endure for ever.   Amen.

Closing

Live together in peace, reprimand the unruly, encourage the timid,
help the weak and be very patient with all men. Be sure that no one
repays a bad turn by a bad turn. Good should be our objective
always among ourselves and the world at large.   Amen.

SECRET FAULTS

Opening

Reading

Psalm 19: 7-14

Who can discern his errors?
Clear thou me from hidden faults. (Psalm 19: 12)

Lord, we know we may appear kind to our friends,
    But only You know how often we are thoughtless and unkind.
Lord, we know we can appear generous to our neighbours,
    But only You know our secret meanness.
Lord, we know we can appear good-tempered to outsiders,
    But only You know how cross and disagreeable we can often
    be.
Lord, we know how seldom we can see our own errors, and we ask
    forgiveness and cleansing for our hidden faults.

Help us O God to live our lives according to Your laws,
Grant us eyes that see the beauty in life,
Grant us ears that hear the good in life,
Grant us feet that bear comfort and joy,
And hearts overflowing with love and thankfulness.
We ask it in the Name of the Lord Jesus, Amen.

Closing

Let the words of our mouths and the thoughts of our hearts be now
and always acceptable in Your sight, O Lord, our rock and our
Redeemer. (Ps. 19: 14) Amen.

REJOICING

Opening   *Reading*

Rejoice in the Lord always; again I will   Philippians 4: 1–9
say, Rejoice. (Phil. 4: 4)

We remember today, Lord, that Your Word commands us to rejoice.

We rejoice in the pure things—a small baby, the unspoiled morning freshness, and kindnesses done with no thought of reward or self-interest.

We rejoice in the lovely things—flowers and trees, small animals, and the happy faces of children and young people.

We rejoice in the just things—the wisdom of our laws, and our nation's care for the widowed, the sick and the poor.

We rejoice in the excellent things, good books, skilful paintings, radio and television programmes that increase our knowledge and enlighten our minds.

But Lord, we rejoice most of all in You, who have given us all these things so that we may enjoy them.   Amen.

Lord, You have told us not to be anxious about anything—But Lord, we are anxious.

We're anxious about our children who are sometimes rude and disobedient.

We're anxious about our parents who need so much of our time and our attention.

We're anxious about money—in case we do not have sufficient.

We're anxious about our time—because there doesn't seem to be enough of it.

Take all our anxieties to Yourself, Lord, and give us instead Your peace and joy.   Amen.

Closing

The peace of God which passes all understanding keep your hearts and minds in Christ Jesus.   Amen.

THE TONGUE

Opening   *Reading*

Who is wise and understanding among you?   James 3: 1–12
By his good life let him show his works
in the meekness of wisdom. (James 3: 13)

O Lord, we confess we talk too much.
  We gossip about other people behind their backs.
  We complain about high food prices, bad weather and our own
    ailments.
  We criticize the way things are done and the people who do them.
  We discuss the shortcomings of our friends and neighbours, often
    despising them because they do not think or act in the way we
    think and act ourselves.
  We exaggerate and minimize, and repeat half-truths, seldom
    stopping to consider what great forests we may be setting
    ablaze by the small fires that we light with our tongues.
Forgive us, Lord, for we need Your forgiveness so much, each and
every one of us.   Amen.

Heavenly Father, we ask that You will take our tongues and use
    them in Your service.
Use them to speak words of comfort and encouragement.
Use them to witness to Your love and faithfulness.
Use them for praise and thanks.
Use them for laughter and merriment.
Use them to soothe and to sympathize,
    That from our mouths may flow all that is good and pure and
true, and a blessing to our fellow men.
    In the name of the Lord Jesus we ask it, Amen.

Closing

Take our tongues and speak through them. Take our hands and
work with them. Take our hearts and set them on fire with love for
You. In Your Name we ask it.   Amen.

LIFE'S GOOD THINGS

Opening   *Reading*

I know that whatever God does endures   Ecclesiastes 3 : 10–15
for ever; nothing can be added to it,
nor anything taken from it. (Ecc. 3 : 14)

O God, You have made the world so beautiful, yet sometimes we
confess we do not see the beauty.

    Birds sing, water murmurs over stones, and leaves make music
       with their rustling, yet we do not stop to listen.

    The softness of a baby's cheek, a kitten's fur, and the smooth feel
       of planed wood, invite our touch, but we are heedless.

    The pleasant sharpness of lemon, the sweetness of honey and the
       hot spiciness of a good curry, do not arouse our thankfulness
       for our sense of taste.

    The smell of a log fire, ground coffee, or a rose in bud, pleases our
       sense of smell, but fails to make us grateful.

It is Your wish that we enjoy ourselves and the gifts that You have
given us. Thank You for giving us the means of enjoyment and
gifts to enjoy, and make us more aware of the little things that can
be a source of continuing joy to all of us.   Amen.

Dear Lord, remind us that—

    Happiness comes from loving,

    Happiness comes from giving,

    Happiness comes from caring,

    Happiness comes from sharing,

    Happiness comes from working,

    Happiness comes from worshipping the One who has shown
the world the only way of true happiness.   Amen.

Closing

Jesus said: "If you keep my commandments you will abide in my
love, just as I have kept my Father's commandments and abide in His
love. These things I have spoken to you, that my joy may be in you,
and that your joy may be full." (John 15 : 10, 11)   Amen.

CHILDREN

Opening   *Reading*

Truly, I say to you, unless you turn and   Matthew 18: 1–6
become like children, you will never
enter the kingdom of heaven. (Matt. 18: 3)

Loving Lord Jesus, We thank You for the children in our families
and the joy they bring us; for their eagerness to learn, for their
energy, and for their innocence.

Lord, grant that we may not become impatient at answering their
questions; that we may not try to suppress their energy; that we
may never be instrumental in destroying their innocence.

Help us to learn from them, and to teach them only those things
that we have proved to be of lasting value.   Amen.

Lord, guard our children from the dangers that beset them on every
side, and help us to give them the right values.

Help us to impress upon them the necessity of telling the truth.

Help us to demonstrate the satisfaction gained from doing a job
well.

Help us to show them that hard work brings its own reward.

Help us to teach them the meaning of real love.

Help us to be honest about our own shortcomings, and to have
the wisdom to introduce our children to the only One who can
uphold and uplift them at all times, Jesus Christ our Lord.
Amen.

Closing

Whatever is true, whatever is honourable, whatever is just, whatever
is pure, whatever is lovely, whatever is gracious, if there is any
excellence, if there is anything worthy of praise, think about these
things. (Phil. 4: 8) And teach them to your children.   Amen.

Opening   *Reading*

And Jesus said to His disciples,   Mark 6: 7–13 & 30–32
"Come away by yourselves to a lonely
place, and rest awhile." For many were
coming and going, and they had no leisure
even to eat. (Mark 6: 31)

Father, we thank You for the happiness of holidays and for the
relaxation and refreshment they bring. We ask that You will
watch over us as we travel and bring us safely to our destination.
We pray that we may not be too dependent on good weather,
but learn to enjoy the wind and the storm as well as sunshine
and blue skies. Remind us to be unselfish; and to be gracious
and courteous to those who wait upon us, so that their task may
be lightened. Give us the spirit of adventure so that we may
taste new foods, meet new people and join in new pursuits to
broaden our horizons and widen our outlook.

All these things we ask in the Name of the Lord Jesus.   Amen.

Lord Jesus Christ, who had time and patience to spend on children
and would not allow Your disciples to send them away, give us
patience with our children during their school holiday and help us
to make time to be with them and share in their games and sports
and hobbies.

Help us to remember that we shall have them for such a small
part of their lives, and that household tasks will still be with us when
they have left home to make their own way in the world.

Grant that we may have the wisdom to make school holidays
times of happiness to be remembered all their lives.   Amen.

Closing

May the Lord refresh and renew you so that, restored in body, mind
and spirit, you may return to your daily tasks strengthened and
invigorated for the months ahead.   Amen.

MONEY

He who sows sparingly will also reap   2 Cor. 9: 6–15
sparingly, and he who sows bountifully
will also reap bountifully. (2 Cor. 9: 6)

Almighty God, we thank You for all the blessings that You have
given us:

A regular and adequate wage.

A warm and comfortable home.

Satisfying meals and a variety of clothes.

Medical and dental care and the provision of medicines we need.

Money for small luxuries and entertainments for our children.

We confess, Father, we often take these things for granted and
complain about the things we don't possess instead of thanking You
for all the bounty that is ours.

Lord, give us grateful hearts, and in the measure we have been
given, so let us give with gladness.   Amen.

Lord, we think of those who are hungry and cold and homeless; of
those who have no job and therefore no wage; of those who are
sick and have no means of obtaining treatment.

Lord, we are full!

Lord, we are warm!

Lord, we have homes!

Lord, we are fit!

Lord, we have sufficient money for our needs and some to
spare!

Lord, open our eyes!

Lord, open our hearts!

Lord, open our purses!

Lord, don't let us sit back in comfort and ignore those in want.
Don't let us, Lord! In Your Name we ask it.   Amen.

Closing

He who supplies seed to the sower and bread for food will supply
and multiply your resources and increase the harvest of your
righteousness. You will be enriched in every way for great generosity
which will produce thanksgiving to God.   Amen.

Opening   *Reading*

Then the Lord God said, "It is not good   Genesis 2: 18–24
that a man should be alone; I will make
him a helper fit for him." (Gen. 2: 18)

Loving Heavenly Father, we thank You for all the joys of happy
marriage. For someone with whom we can share our troubles. For
someone to comfort us when we are sad. For someone to rejoice
with us over our triumphs and to console us over our failures. For
someone to cherish. For someone to cook for and for whom to
make a home.

Lord, forgive us when we grumble about the married state; when
we complain we haven't enough money; when we are quarrelsome
and won't admit we are in the wrong; when we find fault and look
for trouble.

Lord, please help us to work at our marriages and keep them in
good repair. Amen.

Lord, we ask for Your blessing today on those whose marriages are
    broken or unhappy, and for the children of such unions. Where
    there is still hope, Lord, fan again the love that brought them
    together and help them to make a new start. Where there is no
    hope, Lord, strengthen and comfort and surround them with
    Your everlasting love. Give wisdom to those whose job it is to
    advise and bring hope and reason into hopeless and unreasonable
    situations, and grant that both husbands and wives may recog-
    nize their own shortcomings, their partners' virtues, and the
    needs of their children. We ask this in Your Name, Amen.

Closing

"Let us love one another, for love is of God, and he who loves is
born of God and knows God. He who does not love does not know
God; for God is love." (John 4: 7, 8) Lord, teach us to love—not in
word or speech—but in deed and truth.   Amen.

A NEW BABY

For this child I prayed; and the Lord has   1 Samuel 1: 19–28
granted me my petition which I made to him.
Therefore I have lent him to the Lord; as
long as he lives he is lent to the Lord. (1 Sam. 1: 27, 28)

Lord, we rejoice today in the arrival of a new baby to a member of
our group.
Thank You, Lord, for the health and safety of both mother and
child.
(*When appropriate:*
Grant that joy may overcome any resentment or jealousy amongst
the other children, and that the parents may be given wisdom
and patience in welding the family harmoniously together.)
Uphold this new mother when she feels weary through loss of sleep
and help her to reorganize her life to fit in her new commit-
ments with a minimum of strain.
And Lord, show us if and when, and how, we can help her, so that
she may have practical proof of our love and fellowship. Amen.

Heavenly Father, we ask Your special blessing on this baby. Lord,
we long for him (her) to be 'lent to the Lord' for the whole of his
(her) life.
Give to him (her) a seeking mind that will search out the truth; a
loving heart that will inspire him (her) in service to others; and the
gift of enduring faith so that he (she) will never despair.
Help him (her) to be pure and honest and upright in all his (her)
thoughts and words and ways.
And grant that throughout his (her) life, he (she) may serve You
faithfully and fight for the cause of right.   Amen.

Closing

Remind us, Lord, of the responsibilities of motherhood and the
importance of a good example. May we never be guilty in thought,
word or deed of impeding the spiritual progress of the children
committed to our keeping. We ask this in Your Name, Amen.

BEING BUSY

Reading

I said in my heart, God will judge the
righteous and the wicked, for he has
appointed a time for every matter, and
for every work. (Ecc. 3: 17)

Ecclesiastes 3: 1-8

Lord, most of us have arrived here today in a rush because we have
been so busy. We stayed in bed too late this morning. We
have gossiped on the phone. We have glanced at the scan-
dal columns of the newspaper. We have dawdled over a
cup of coffee with a friend. We have lingered over our shop-
ping, looking longingly in shop windows at things we can't
afford to buy. We "dithered" over tackling an unpleasant job.
We cleaned and dusted rooms that didn't really need it.

Lord, we know none of these things are wrong in themselves, but
they do take time.

Forgive us, Lord, for complaining that we haven't time, when the
truth is that we are too busy about the wrong things.   Amen.

Almighty God, help us:

To plan our days wisely.

To find time to pray and to read Your Word.

To find time for those who need us most.

To run our homes efficiently, using our energies in the best
ways.

To find time to improve our education and to broaden our
knowledge, and for exercise and recreation.

Teach us to review each day and to be honest in deciding if it has
been well spent.

We ask this in the name of the Lord Jesus, who spent His time
mindful of eternity.   Amen.

Closing

Lord, grant that we spend our time wisely in this life, remembering
that we are preparing ourselves for the life to come. For Your
Name's sake, Amen.

CHRISTMAS

Let us go over to Bethlehem and see   Luke 2: 1–16
this thing that has happened, which
the Lord has made known to us. (Luke 2: 15)

Dear Heavenly Father, we bring before You today all those who
    wait for the birth of their child.
  We think of those who are too poor to prepare for it properly.
  We think of those who have no home in which to rear it com-
    fortably.
  We think of women who have no husband to stand by them and
    cherish them, and must face the responsibilities of motherhood
    alone.
Grant Your protection, O Lord, to those who need it most, and at
this season of rejoicing and goodwill, may we with generous hearts
reflect our love for the Christ Child in our love to young babies and
their parents. In Your Name we ask it, Amen.

Loving Lord, we ask Your blessing on those who love and care for
    children who are not their own; Kindly step-parents, Foster
    mothers and fathers, Those who work in hospitals and chil-
    dren's homes, and Those who educate and look after children
    who are crippled or mentally retarded.
Give them joy in their work, and strength and courage for each
day, Amen.

Help us this Christmas-tide, good Lord, to take more joy in giving
than receiving, in loving than being loved, so that the true spirit of
this joyful season may fill our hearts and our homes and overflow to
everyone we meet.   Amen.

Glory to God in the Highest
And on earth peace among men with
whom He is pleased. (Luke 2: 14)   Amen.

Opening   *Reading*

Do not be afraid; for I know that you seek   Matthew 28: 1–10
Jesus who was crucified. He is not here;
for he is risen, as he said. (Matt. 28: 5)

Dear Father God, We rejoice in this season of hope which reminds
us of the reality of our faith, and the certainty of life after death. Yet
we are often doubtful and faithless. We grieve over our loved ones
who have gone before, and fear lest we shall never see them again.
We are slothful and cowardly about advertising our faith, forgetful
that by our silence we are denying others the advantages that we
ourselves enjoy. We fear death, because we prefer the limitations of
our present existence to the limitless potential of the world un-
known.

Lord, you broke the barrier between life and death.

You proved that death is not the end, but the beginning.

Renew and strengthen our faith, Lord, at this Easter time.
Amen.

Lord, the bulbs we buried in the ground in the autumn have grown
into beautiful flowers.

The trees which have stood stark and bare throughout the
winter are bursting into leaf.

The chrysalis which has lain dormant during the cold months
will soon crack and allow the butterfly to escape. Accept our
praise for the renewal of life that can be found in You! Amen.

Closing

"Thus it is written, that the Christ should suffer and on the third day
rise from the dead, and that repentance and forgiveness of sins
should be preached in His name to all nations. . . . You are witnesses
of these things." (Luke 24: 46–48.) Go now and obey His command.
Amen.

WHITSUN

Opening   *Reading*

Opening   *Reading*

And in the last days it shall be, God   Acts 2: 1–12
declares, that I will pour out my Spirit
upon all flesh, and your sons and your
daughters shall prophesy, and your young
men shall see visions, and your old men
shall dream dreams. (Acts 2: 17)

O Lord, grant us the power of Your Holy Spirit in our lives even
    as you have promised.
Remove from our hearts and minds and lives those things which
    hinder,
And increase and nourish all that is good.
    Give us courage to speak for You,
Energy to work for You,
    And strength to face the troubles of each day.
So that, through us, Your Kingdom may increase and Your Name
    be glorified.   Amen.

Loving Lord Jesus, take our group and transform it by the power of
Your Holy Spirit so that all our members may work together for
the cause of love.

Take our Church and revive it with Your Holy Spirit, so that all
who worship there may become vitally concerned for the spiritual
health of their neighbours, their families and their friends.

Take our town and grant that its affairs may be ordered by those
who are Your servants, directed by Your Spirit's power.

Take our nation and forgive us where we need forgiveness, and
give us a longing to live under Your laws and subject to Your
Spirit's will.

In Your Name we ask it, Amen.

Closing

Lord, You have made known to us the way of life. Fill us full of
gladness with Your presence.   Amen.

Opening   *Reading*

Blessed shall be your basket and your kneading   Deut. 28: 1–9
trough. Blessed shall you be when you come in,
and blessed shall you be when you go out.
(Deut. 28: 5, 6)

We thank You, O God, for all the joys of harvest time.
 For the satisfaction we gain from making jam and jelly and
 chutney and preserving and freezing tomatoes, fruit and
 vegetables.
 For the beauty of the fields of ripe corn and the tints of autumn
 leaves.
 For the smell of wood fires and ripe apples.
 For the feel of a crisp morning and dry leaves crunching under
 our feet.
 For these and many other blessings, accept our grateful thanks,
 O Lord.   Amen.

O Lord, Our thoughts go out to the many women of other lands
whose baskets are empty.
 Our hearts are touched with pity as we think of mothers sur-
rounded by hungry children whom they have no means of feeding.
 We share in the distress they suffer as they send their menfolk out
to work on an empty stomach.
 Grant that our pity may show itself in giving so that we may play
our part in relieving the needs of those who are hungry.   Amen.

Closing

Establish us, O Lord, as a people holy to Yourself, and help us to
keep Your commandments and walk in Your ways.   Amen.
(Adapted from Deut. 28: 9)

ANNUAL GENERAL MEETING

Opening

Reading

Therefore, brethren, pick out from among
you seven men of good repute, full of the
Spirit and of wisdom, whom we may appoint
to this duty. (Acts 6: 3)

Acts 6: 1–7

Lord, we need Your guidance especially today as we meet to
appoint our committee and officers for the coming year. Help
us to choose the right people for the right jobs. Restrain us from
choosing people just because they are our friends without
considering their capabilities.

Show us clearly those who will be of greatest spiritual strength to
our group.

Indicate new people who may have a great deal to offer but are shy
about putting themselves forward.

Give those of our members who may have served for many years
the courage to step back if they feel it is right to do so.

Lord, we long for this group to be greatly used in Your service.
Take it now and mould it as You will.   Amen.

Almighty God, it is fitting at this time to re-dedicate ourselves to
You. Father, clarify our aims; help us to examine honestly our past
record; increase the spirit of love and friendliness in our group;
teach us the value of united prayer. Give us a real concern for the
lonely, the sick and the underprivileged. Forbid it, Father, that we
should meet together just for a social gathering, heedless of our
higher calling as ambassadors of Your Kingdom. We beseech You
to show us what to do and how to do it.   Amen.

Closing

We thank You, Lord, because we believe You have guided us in our
business today. Bless the appointed members of our committee and
help them to have wisdom and sound judgement, and give to all of
us a spirit of loyalty and enthusiasm and a determination to support
them in their decisions.   Amen.

Opening   *Reading*

But, according to his promise, we wait   2 Peter 3 : 8–14
for new heavens and a new earth in which
righteousness dwells. (2 Pet. 3 : 13)

Lord, as we come before You today, our first meeting of a New
     Year, we ask for Your forgiveness for the past and Your
     blessing and encouragement for the future.
Forgive us for the opportunities we have not taken.
Forgive us for the prayers we have not prayed.
Forgive us for the people we have not visited.
Forgive us for lack of faith, for lack of patience, for lack of efficiency,
     both in our homes and in our group.
We thank You, Lord, that we can put these things behind us and
reach out to new opportunities in this New Year. Help us right from
the beginning, Lord, and be with us to the end.   Amen.

Almighty God, We approach this New Year in a spirit of adventure.
We do not know what it will hold for us—but You know.
We do not know how many new members will be added to us, and
     who they will be—but You know.
We do not know which members will leave us and for what
     reasons—but You know.
We do not know the speakers who will particularly challenge and
     stimulate us, and in what fields—but You know.
We do not know in what ways we shall be called to work for You,
     and how willing and able we shall prove to be—but You know.
Lord, help us to be enthusiastic and joyful in Your service and at
peace with You, with ourselves and with our fellow-men. We ask
it in the name of the Lord Jesus.   Amen.

Closing

Grant that we may live lives of holiness and godliness, and be
zealous, without spot of blemish, and at peace.   Amen.

27

GROUP BIRTHDAY

You shall therefore keep all the commandment   Deut. 11: 8–15
which I command you this day, that you may
be strong, and go in and take possession of
the land which you are going over to possess. (Deut. 11: 8)

Lord, You know that today is the birthday of our group. We thank
You that we have been brought safely through another year. We
thank You for those who have led the group, and for those who
have supported them; for the new members who have joined us, and
we think of the friends who have left us. We thank You for the
speakers who have widened our knowledge and deepened our faith.
We ask Your blessings on the new babies born to our members and
for Your watchful care over any older children who have left home.
Give us continuing love and care for each other and a readiness to
include newcomers into our group.
We ask this in Your Name, Amen.

Almighty God, As we prepare to go forward into a new year, give
us Your wisdom and Your strength. Open our minds to new ideas
and modern methods. Help us to keep the things that are good and
useful, and discard what is dated and useless. Give those who have
something to offer confidence and courage to serve on our committee. Save us from getting into a rut and wanting to stay there.
Guard us from the danger of allowing social projects to take pre-
cedence over spiritual ones. Show us how we can attract outsiders
and retain their interest. And, most of all, grant that each one of us
may live a life worthy of You and the high calling to which You
have called us.   Amen.

Closing

Help us, O Lord, to lay up Your words in our hearts and souls, and
teach them to our children, talking to them when we are sitting in
our homes, when we are walking by the way, when we lie down and
when we rise, so that You may be with us wherever we go.   Amen.

WOMEN'S WORLD DAY OF PRAYER

Opening

Reading

In praying do not heap up empty phrases
as the Gentiles do; for they think that
they will be heard for their many words.
Do not be like them, for your Father knows
what you need before you ask him.

Matthew 6: 5–15

Pray then like this: Our Father who art in heaven, Hallowed be thy name. Thy kingdom come, Thy will be done, On earth as it is in heaven. Give us this day our daily bread; And forgive us our debts, As we also have forgiven our debtors; And lead us not into temptation, But deliver us from evil. (Matt. 6: 7–13.) Amen.

Almighty God,
   We unite today with women everywhere to pray for the whole
      world.
   We know that the sin and suffering that abound have been
      brought upon ourselves through our own wilfulness and dis-
      obedience.   Lord, forgive us.
   We confess that we have valued wealth and possessions above
      spiritual gifts, and we have failed to love other people as our-
      selves.   Lord, forgive us.
   The unrest and greed of our nations reflect the unrest and greed
      in our individual hearts.   Lord, forgive us.
   We pray for a renewed sense of responsibility in us and in all
      mankind.   Grant this, O Lord.
   We pray for a transforming love, in man, for man.
                                                    Grant this, O Lord.
   We pray for a fresh determination to obey Your commandments.
                                                    Grant this, O Lord.
   We pray for new values, new outlooks and new priorities.
                                                    Grant this, O Lord.
And in the coming days fill our hearts and homes with Your Holy
Spirit and give us Your peace.   Amen.

Closing

Lord, we have asked—give to us. We have knocked—open to us.
We have sought—grant that we may find You and help others to
find You too.   Amen.

A MEMBER LEAVING

Opening   *Reading*

And now I commend you to God and to the   Acts 20: 28–38
word of his grace, which is able to build
you up and to give you the inheritance
among all those who are sanctified. (Acts 20: 32)

Father, We are sad today because one of our friends is leaving us.
Thank You for the work she has done amongst us, for the friendship
she has given us, for the love she has shown us.

Sustain her in the upheaval of moving house and remaking a
home in a new place. Give her safe conduct on the journey. Challenge her with the new opportunities that lie ahead. Prepare a place
for her in the Church where she will worship, so that her talents and
abilities may be fully used.

And may the knowledge of our love for her go with her and
remain with her in the days ahead.

In the Name of the Lord Jesus we ask it.   Amen.

Remind us, O Lord, that "here we have no continuing city but we
seek one to come". Grant that we do not lose sight of the temporary
nature of our homes and possessions and become too attached to
them. Help us to keep a light hold upon material things and to hold
fast those things that are of everlasting worth.

Give us a greater concern for the spiritual welfare of our friends
so that our relationship with them can never be broken either by
distance or by death itself.

These things we ask in Jesus' Name, Amen.

Closing

To God's love and mercy we now commit ourselves, beseeching
Him to keep us steadfast in the faith that we may bear a good
witness to our Lord and Saviour wherever we may go.   Amen.

WORSHIP

Opening   *Reading*

"I am the bread of life; he who comes to me   John 6: 35–48
shall not hunger, and he who believes in me
shall never thirst." (John 6: 35)

Lord, we have come together again today and yet we hardly know
what has drawn us. For some of us it is the pleasure of meeting and
talking with our friends. Some of us have been drawn by a sense of
duty or responsibility. Some of us come from habit.

But Lord, now we are here, use this meeting for our spiritual
growth.

May our singing be wholehearted praise.

May our prayers be simple conversation with You.

May our talk deepen our fellowship with each other.

May our giving be generous and willing.

For Your dear sake, we ask it, Amen.

Almighty God, grant us now freedom from the cares and duties of
the day, as we bow our heads before You and fill our minds
with thoughts of You.

Forgive us for unkind words and actions   (*pause*)

Accept our thanks for all Your goodness to us   (*pause*)

Be near those who are sad and suffering   (*pause*)

And feed our souls with the Living Bread.   Amen.

Closing

Come with us as we return to our homes, O Lord, and grant that
what we have learned from You today may take root and grow in
our hearts and lives to Your Glory.   Amen.

OUR MINISTER AND THOSE WHO HELP HIM

Opening   *Reading*

Grace is given to each of us according to   Ephesians 4: 1–7 &
the measure of Christ's gift. . . . And his   11–16
gifts were that some should be apostles,
some prophets, some evangelists, some
pastors and teachers. (Eph. 4: 7 & 11)

Lord, we pray today for the one whom You have set in this place
     to minister to our spiritual needs.
Lord, he needs to give out so much love—fill him continually with
     Your love.
Lord, he needs boundless physical energy—keep him in good health.
Lord, he comes face to face with so much sorrow and pain and
     bereavement—sustain him, we pray.
Lord, he must have so much understanding—give him Your
     wisdom.   We ask this in Your Name.   Amen.

Remind us today, O God, that the Church is the body of Christ and
we are members of it.

     We pray for those who carry the main burdens of responsibility
(our minister, curates, lady worker, Sunday School Superintendent,
M.U. enrolling member, Wives Group leader, Youth Club leader
etc.)   *(pause)*

     For the members of our council (or committee)who deal with the
business side of Church life.   *(pause)*

     For those who clean the church and arrange the flowers, for those
who organize refreshments and paint posters or decorate the building
for special occasions.   *(pause)*
Show us the special job we have to do for You in our Church, Lord,
and help us to do it willingly and efficiently.   Amen.

Closing

Look carefully then how you walk, not as unwise men but as wise,
making the most of the time because the days are evil. Therefore do
not be foolish, but understand what the will of the Lord is. (Eph. 5:
15–17.) May He help you to do it.   Amen.

MISSIONARY WORK

Opening   *Reading*

"Lo, I am with you always, to the   Matthew 28: 16–20
close of the age." (Matt. 28: 20)

Lord, You have told us to teach others of You but we have not
taught them. We have let others go and teach, and have for-
gotten even to pray for them, or to give them our support.
Forgive us, Lord.
Lord, we pray for them now.
    We pray for the women who have left families and homes and
friends in order to obey Your commandment. We know they
have given up many of the little things that go to making a
woman's life—a visit to the hairdresser, a walk around the
shops, a cup of coffee in a restaurant with a friend. We know
they have given up many big things—close family ties, a comfortable home and sometimes the opportunity of being a wife
and mother.
Give them Your inward joy and peace, Lord.
Keep them in good health and soundness of mind.
Show them fruit in their work and may they be conscious of the
prayer of Christian people at home, so that they do not feel lonely
in the work to which You have called them.   Amen.

Almighty God, Help us to be missionaries in the place in which we
live; to our families, living out day by day the faith we profess;
to our neighbours, always ready to listen to their troubles and
to offer our help; to our tradesmen, showing by our patience
and courtesy the grace of Christ; to our friends, sharing their
joys and respecting their confidences with unfailing love and
loyalty.
   Father, we know we're not really worthy—but please use us just
the same.   Amen.

Closing

Lord, help us to remember constantly, to give freely and con-
sistently, to pray and to write regularly, so that we may share in
Your work of the world's redemption.   Amen.

OTHER CHURCHES

Opening

Reading

And this is eternal life, that they may know thee the only true God, and Jesus Christ whom thou has sent. (John 17: 3)

John 17: 20–26

Father in heaven, we thank You for the reminder that we are all one in Christ Jesus. No differences in buildings or forms of service can alter this fact. Lord, bring us ever closer together and make us more eager for this one-ness.

The world will never accept our witness until it is a united witness to Your saving and keepingpo wer. Lord, save us from wrangling over petty differences, and becoming indifferent to the crying need of a world that is trying to live without You!

Lord, help us to recognize the different qualities that are seen in different Churches with different forms of worship.

We thank You for—the discipline of the Roman Catholic Church; the obedience of the Baptist Church; the sincerity of the Methodist Church; the simplicity of the Congregational Church; the endurance of the Anglican Church; the enthusiasm of the Pentecostal Church; and the faithfulness to the Word of God shown by the Plymouth Brethren.

Lord, help us to learn from each other, and to worship You in truth and unity. Amen.

We thank You, Lord, for the one who has come to speak to us today. Use him (her) to give us greater understanding and a broader outlook. Bless the Church from which he (she) has come and the one who is responsible for the ministry there. Show us ways in which we can work together for the strengthening and extension of Your kingdom on earth. Amen.

Closing

Almighty and everlasting God, bind us together in Your love so that our love towards each other and our unity with each other may witness to Your saving and keeping power. In Christ's Name we ask it, Amen.

SAMARITANS

Opening   *Reading*

You shall love the Lord your God with all   Luke 10: 30–37
your heart, and with all your soul, and with
all your strength, and with all your mind;
and your neighbour as yourself . . . do this
and you will live. (Luke 10: 27, 28)

Lord Jesus Christ, bless, we beseech You, all those who work for You through the Samaritan service.

Give them courage when faced with people whose despair has made them dangerous and unbalanced; help them not to be overwhelmed by the troubles and depressions of those whom they seek to help; grant them patience to be good listeners and Divine wisdom as they offer advice.

  Grant, O Lord, that
    As they give strength, so they may find strength,
    As they give comfort, they may find comfort,
    As they give help, so they may be helped.
    We ask this in Your Name. Amen.

Almighty God,
    We pray for all those who have found the burdens and difficulties of this life too much for them. We think of those who contemplate suicide—reach out to them, Lord. We think of those who are unmarried and are to bear a child and are frightened of the consequences of their guilt—comfort them, Lord. We think of those in financial difficulties and who cannot see a way out—help them to get things in proportion, Lord, We think of the old and the lonely and the unwanted—show them how they can contribute to life, Lord. Lord, all these are Your children—touch them and make them whole. Amen.

Closing

Lord, open our eyes to the need of others and, if it is Your will that we should offer ourselves to the Samaritan service, make it very plain to us and give us courage to answer Your call. Bless those who serve You and those who are served. For your Name's sake, Amen.

FLOWER ARRANGERS

Opening   *Reading*

Now there are varieties of gifts, but the   I Cor. 12: 27–31a
same Spirit; and there are varieties of
service, but the same Lord; and there are
varieties of working but it is the same
God who inspires them all in every one.
(I Cor. 12: 4–6)

We thank You, dear Lord, for the beauty of flowers and the
     pleasure they give to us.
Thank You for the gift of a child's posy gathered from the woods
     and hedgerows.
Thank You for the bunches of flowers given as a love-token.
Thank You for the bowls and vases of flowers that make our homes
     gay.
Thank You for the flowers that beautify our Church week by week,
     and the hands that arrange them. Amen.

Loving Heavenly Father, please bless the members of our flower
guild (or rota) whose work is so often taken for granted.
As they work alone in the Church each weekend in order to make
Your house more beautiful, may they feel You very near them.
Remind us to support their work and to thank them for it, and
grant that the beauty of the arrangements that they create may be
a constant reminder of You, who created all things. Amen.

Closing

Help us, O Lord, to consider carefully the gifts that have been given
to us, and show us how we can best use them in Your service and
to Your glory. Amen.

WOMEN IN PUBLIC OFFICE

Opening

Reading

Trust in the Lord with all your heart,
and do not rely on your own insight.
In all your ways acknowledge him and
he will make straight your paths. (Prov. 3: 5, 6)

Proverbs 2: 1–8

Lord, guide and direct those women who have been called to public office: our women Members of Parliament, council members, magistrates and school governors. Grant them wisdom to discern between right and wrong, justice and injustice, progress and retreat. Grant them courage to stand alone when necessary. May they never become so involved in service to the community that they have no time to consider the problems and concerns of the individual. Help them to listen patiently as well as to speak forcefully, and keep them fit and sound in body, mind and spirit.

We ask this in Your Name, Amen.

Almighty and Everlasting God,
Grant to each one of us a healthy interest in the administration of the affairs of our town (village, city) and country.
Where we have a vote, Lord, help us to use it wisely. Where we have a chance to serve on a committee, help us not to shirk responsibility. Where we have the opportunity to attend a public meeting, save us from lethargy.
We know how often we grumble and complain of injustices but lack the energy and interest to try to put them right.
We know how often we criticize others for the action they have taken but take no action ourselves.
Stir us up to put our Christian faith into action and our Christian love into service. Amen.

Closing

Lord, convict those of us who are lazy. Direct those of us who are unsure. Open up opportunities for those of us who are willing and encourage those who are already serving You in public life, that, with Your help we may shoulder our responsibilities and seek to serve our fellow-men. Amen.

RADIO AND TELEVISION

Opening

Reading

An intelligent mind acquires knowledge,
and the ear of the wise seeks knowledge.
(Prov. 18: 15)

Proverbs 18: 4–15

Almighty God, who has given man the power to reason and discover
and invent, we lay before You in prayer today, Lord, our television
and radio sets. Guide those amongst the administrators, producers
and script writers, actors, announcers and newscasters, who are Your
servants, in the work to which You have called them. Help them to
be an influence for good in their various spheres. May they stand
firm against the temptation to lower their standards. May they never
allow their judgement to be perverted.

Remind them of the tremendous responsibility that has been
given to them and the far-reaching effects of their decisions, and may
they be guided by Your Holy Spirit in their work. We ask this in
Your Name, Amen.

Almighty God,

Teach us discernment as we listen to our radio and watch our
television sets. Save us from becoming hardened to violence and
brutality. Grant that we may not find cause for laughter in things
that are cruel or obscene. Give us increased appreciation of fine
music, good plays and informative documentary programmes,
and a healthy and untainted sense of humour, so that we may
enjoy what is good and switch off what is unprofitable for our
mental and spiritual development.   Amen.

Closing

Help us, O Lord, to test everything, hold fast what is good, and
abstain from every form of evil; and may the God of peace Himself
sanctify us wholly, and may our spirits, souls and bodies be kept
sound and blameless until the coming of our Lord Jesus Christ.
(1 Thess. 5: 21–23)   Amen.

Wash yourselves; make yourselves clean;
remove the evil of your doings from before
my eyes; cease to do evil, learn to do good;
seek justice, correct oppression; defend the
fatherless, plead for the widow. (Isa. 1: 16, 17)

Almighty God, We long for the time when wars shall end, but
know this time will never come until all men realize that the
way of Christ is the only way of true peace.
We pray for all those who are the victims of war:
For those whose homes have been destroyed;
For little children who have been left fatherless and motherless;
For the wounded who have suffered terrible disfigurement or the
loss of a limb;
For those who have lost husband, and father, and children, and all
they hold most dear;
For those who have lost their means of livelihood;
For those who have become mentally unbalanced;
For those whose faith has been shaken.
Grant that Your Spirit may enlighten the minds of leaders and
statesmen, so that they may see the uselessness of violence, and
the wisdom of settling world affairs across the conference table.
Amen.

Lord, we pray for peace in our families that petty quarrelling may
cease; for peace in our homes that love may overrule; for peace in
our organizations, that all may work for the common good; for
peace in the world, that greed and aggression may be overcome; for
peace in each and every one of us, so that the peace we have in You
may overflow to others.   Amen.

Closing

Jesus said: "Peace I leave with you; my peace I give to you; not as
the world gives do I give to you. Let not your hearts be troubled,
neither let them be afraid. . . . Rise and let us go hence." (John 14:
27–31)

FOR VICTIMS OF AN ACCIDENT

For as we share abundantly in Christ's   2 Cor. 1: 3–11
sufferings, so through Christ we share
abundantly in comfort too. (2 Cor. 1: 5)

Lord, today our thoughts are with those who have suffered as a
result of the air (road, train) accident.

We pray for the mothers and wives and sisters of those who have
died, asking that Your comfort and love will surround them.

We pray for the children left fatherless or motherless or orphaned,
and for those who will care for them.

We pray for those who feel responsible for the accident, that You
will sustain them.

We pray for the doctors and nurses who are caring for the
injured, that their work may be inspired by Your divine compassion.

You suffered, O Lord, so we know You understand their suffering.
Amen.

Heavenly Father, We know that all who pass through life are called
upon to endure their share of suffering. Help us to use our experience for the good of the world.

If we suffer ill health, make us patient with those who are ill. If
we have suffered bereavement, make us gentle with those who
have lost a dear one. If we have suffered material hardship, make
us sympathetic with those who are poor or homeless. If we are
lonely, help us to seek out those who need our company.

So that in comforting others we may ourselves be comforted.
Amen.

Closing

Grant that we may be able to comfort those who are in any affliction,
with the comfort with which we ourselves are comforted by God.
Amen.

FOR YOUNG PEOPLE IN TROUBLE

Have mercy on us, O God,   Psalm 51: 1–10
according to Your steadfast love;
according to Your abundant mercy
blot out our transgressions. (Ps. 51: 1)

Heavenly Father, our thoughts and prayers are turned today towards
the young people of our country who are following the broad
and easy way that leads only to destruction.

We think of those who are taking drugs in order to induce a false
and temporary feeling of happiness; of those who are leading
immoral lives in a fruitless search for the meaning of true love;
of those who steal because they hope that material things will
satisfy; of those who have lost their personal respect and have
become dirty and degraded in body and mind.

Father, we know You love these young people and yearn over
them. Help us to love them too and to understand and some-
how meet their desperate Need. In the Name of the Lord Jesus
we ask it.   Amen.

We ask You, O Lord, to give wisdom to those of us who are
mothers or are in some way responsible for the welfare and
training of children and young people.

Lord, we are frightened of the responsibility!

Lord, we know we are not wise enough for the task!

Lord, we fall ourselves, so how can we hope to help them stand
upright?

Lord, we give in to temptation, so how can we teach them to stand
firm?

Lord, we are so often unloving, so how can they learn from us the
true meaning of love?

Use us merely as channels for Your wisdom and love and
strength for we know that alone we can do nothing.   Amen.

Closing

Cast your burden on the Lord and He will sustain you; He will
never permit the righteous to be moved. (Ps. 55: 22)   Amen.

MARCHES AND RIOTS

Opening   *Reading*

Fight the good fight of the faith;   1 Tim. 6: 1–11
take hold of the eternal life to
which you were called when you made
the good confession in the presence
of many witnesses. (1 Tim. 6: 12)

Almighty God, We would pray today for those who take part in
   marches and riots and demonstrations of every kind, and for
   the causes that lie at the root of them.

    We pray that the leaders may have wisdom and discernment,
and may not be influenced by the wrong motives.

    We pray that those who follow may only do so from con-
viction and not solely in order to be one of the crowd.

    We pray that violence may be kept in check and people's
property respected.

    We pray that law and order may be regarded and personal
resentment kept in check.

    We pray that men may come to see that peaceful settlements
must always be the aim of those who follow the teaching of
Christ, and seek to live according to His will.   Amen.

Lord, we pray for the young people whose sense of injustice can
   often be roused more easily than our own. Foster their love for
   their fellow-men. Clarify their thinking and use their enthusiasm and energy aright.

Forgive us when we have failed to give them a right lead, and
grant that where we have lost opportunities they may find
them.

Help them to a right understanding of the world's needs and
protect them from corruption.

    All this we ask in Jesus's Name, Amen.

Closing

Help us, O God, to guard what has been entrusted to us, and to
avoid the godless chatter and contradictions of what is sometimes
falsely called knowledge, for we know that, by professing it, some
have missed the mark as regards the faith.   Amen.

Opening	*Reading*
	Mark 1: 29–42

I was hungry and you gave me food,
I was thirsty and you gave me drink,
I was a stranger and you welcomed me,
I was naked and you clothed me,
I was sick and you visited me. . . .
Truly, I say to you, as you did it to one of the
least of these my brethren, you did it to me. (Matt. 25: 35–40)

Loving Lord Jesus, You spent much of Your time on earth healing sick bodies and bringing health to troubled minds, bless, we pray You, all those who are continuing Your work in clinics and hospitals throughout the world.

Give inspiration to those who are seeking to discover new drugs to combat crippling and mortal diseases.

Give courage and endurance to those who care for the chronically sick.

Give skill to the hands and brains of surgeons as they perform delicate operations, and

Give stamina and compassion to the nurses who play such a valuable part in the comfort and recovery of all sick people. In Your Name we ask it, Amen.

Almighty God, We pray today for any of our group who are, at this time in hospital, (especially . . .) If they are frightened, reassure them. If they are in pain, relieve them. If they are homesick, comfort them. If they are lonely, help them to make friends.

And grant that we, who are well, may not be so full of our own concerns that we fail to write to them, or visit them.   Amen.

Closing

Lord of the loving heart, may ours be loving too. Lord of the gentle hands, may ours be gentle too. Lord of the willing feet, may ours be willing too. So may we grow more like to You in all we say and do. (Adapted from Phyllis Garlick.)   Amen.

FOR THOSE IN SPIRITUAL NEED

Teach me to do thy will, for thou art my God!   Psalm 142: 1–7
Let thy good spirit lead me on a level path!
(Ps. 143: 10)

Loving and merciful Father,
> We would pray for all those who are, at this time, fighting a
> battle of the spirit.
> We pray for those who have lost a dear one and cannot find
> comfort.
> We pray for those who have lost a job and cannot find re-
> assurance.
> We pray for those who see someone suffering and can see no
> purpose in it.
> We pray for those who feel spiritually dry and can find no
> refreshment.

Lord, comfort and reassure and refresh them, and may they be
conscious of Your presence in them, and with them, and around
them in the time of their need. Because we ask it in Jesus' Name,
Amen.

Lord, if we are bitter, sweeten us;
> if we are rebellious, reason with us;
> if we are resentful, be understanding with us;
> if we are sad, comfort us;
> if we are downcast, lift us up;
> if we are doubtful, reassure us.

Lord, we need You.
Meet our need, we pray You.   Amen.

Closing

The steps of a man are from the Lord, and he establishes him in
whose way he delights; though he fall, he shall not be cast headlong,
for the Lord is the stay of his hand. (Ps. 37: 23, 24)   Amen.

                                                Reading

Jesus said, "I am the resurrection and the   John 11: 14–27
life; he who believes in me, though he die,
yet shall he live, and whoever lives and
believes in me shall never die.
Do you believe this?" (John 11: 25, 26)

Lord Jesus Christ, who shares in all our sorrows as well as our joys, we pray today for those who mourn the loss of someone they love.

Lord, You have promised that those who believe in You shall live again. Remind them of Your promise.

Lord, You rose again to prove what You said was true. Help them to hold on to this fact.

Lord, You are the comforter of the sad, the protector of the frightened, the constant companion of the lonely. Lord, make Your presence real to them.

And Lord, we pray that our love may penetrate their grief so that they may let us share it, so that, in sharing, the load may be lightened.

This we pray in Your Name.   Amen.

Loving Heavenly Father,
Grant that present grief and sorrow may not make us unmindful of past blessings and future joys. In spite of pain and suffering, the world is a beautiful place. Flowers bloom, and die, and bloom again. Seeds are dropped into the ground and soon the shoots of new life appear. Old people die but babies are born, and the life cycle goes on.
Father, help us to see ourselves as a small unit of a Divine plan, for now we can only see "in part". When we see You "face to face" we shall understand the reason for our suffering and its part in our spiritual growth and development.   Amen.

Closing

Let us love one another with true affection. Never flagging in zeal, but aglow with the Spirit, serving the Lord. Let us rejoice in our hope, being patient in tribulation and constant in prayer. (Adapted from Rom. 12: 10–12.) In Jesus' Name, Amen.

SPRING

For as the earth brings forth its shoots,
and as a garden causes what is sown in it
to spring up, so the Lord God will cause
righteousness and praise to spring forth
before all the nations. (Isa. 61: 11)

Father, we thank You for the beauty of springtime.

For the soft air, blue skies and warm spring sunshine.

For trees bursting into leaf and golden daffodils in our parks and gardens.

For birds singing in blossoming trees and the pale green tips on the fir trees.

For the urge to spring-clean; the smell of newly washed curtains and clean carpets, and the sparkle of fresh paint.

For the energy to turn out cupboards and polish furniture and wash blankets and mattress covers, and hang them on the line.

For the challenge to remake our gardens and redecorate our homes, and the satisfaction and pleasure we get from our work.

Father, for all these blessings of the springtime, we thank You. Amen.

Help us, dear Lord, to put forth new shoots in our lives. Cleanse us of the sin that can so effectively obscure our Christian witness. Give us fresh energy to work for You, and a fresh challenge to become more like You; and grant that the power of Your Holy Spirit may fill us with a new and lasting zeal. In Your Name we ask it, Amen.

Closing

Grant, Almighty God, that we may be the shoot of Your planting, and the work of Your hands, so that in all we say and do You may be glorified. Amen.

Opening

The earth brought forth vegetation, plants
yielding seed according to their own kinds,
and trees bearing fruit in which is their
seed, each according to its kind. And God
saw that it was good. (Gen. 1: 12)

Father,

We thank You for the summer time; for the loveliness of roses
and the delicacy of sweet peas and gay garden borders edged
with lobelia and alyssum and pansies.

We thank You for the fun of eating out of doors and the bliss of
lazing in a deck chair drenched in sunshine.

We thank You for the summer fruits, for strawberries and rasp-
berries, and the sharp tang of blackcurrants and gooseberries;
for summer vegetables, new peas, tender lettuces and crisp
young carrots.

We thank You for the long evenings and the joy of dewfresh
summer mornings; for blue skies and soft warm breezes and the
freshness of the air after a shower.

The world is good, Lord. Give us eyes that can see the goodness,
Amen.

Lord, give us thought for others in this summer season.

Lord, remind us of someone who would enjoy sharing in a family
picnic.

Lord, show us someone who would appreciate a gift of fruit or
flowers.

Lord, lead us to think of someone without a garden who would
welcome the chance to sit for a while in ours.

Lord, suggest to us the name of a child whom we can take upon a
swimming outing.

Lord, we have so much. Help us to share what we have with those
less fortunate than ourselves.   Amen.

Closing

As the sunshine gives fresh life and health to those it shines upon, so
may we shed abroad the life and health we draw from the One who
is the source of all power, our Saviour Jesus Christ.   Amen.

ON A WET DAY

Opening   *Reading*

He it is who makes the clouds rise at   Psalm 135: 1–7
the end of the earth, who makes lightnings
for the rain and brings forth the wind from
his storehouses. (Ps. 135: 7)

Lord, it is a wet and miserable day, and many of us have been sorely
    tempted to stay by our own firesides rather than brave the
    weather. We thank You, Lord, that we overcame the tempta-
    tion and are here. We thank You for strong boots and shoes, the
    protection of macintoshes and the convenience of cars. Lord, our
    hearts go out to those who do not possess suitable clothing to
    keep out the rain. We thank You for the dry homes from which
    we have come. Lord, our hearts go out to the homeless, and
    those with leaking roofs and windows stuffed up with paper.
Lord, the drains and gutterings of our streets and buildings carry the
    water away. We think of those to whom continual rain means
    flooding, breaking of dams, and consequent turmoil and misery.
Lord, what a little sacrifice we have made in coming here today!
    Forgive us if we thought it was a great one!   Amen.

Lord, teach us to recognize the joys of a wet day: the freshness of the
    air and the cleanliness of the streets that will follow; the fun of
    watching small children in wellingtons jumping in puddles, and
    ducks revelling in the rain; the beauty of raindrops chasing each
    other down the window panes and glistening on a flower or a
    spider's web; the glory of the rainbow and the message it
    brings; the smell of wet earth as it soaks up the life-giving
    moisture; the satisfaction of welcoming home our wet family
    and giving them dry clothes and hot drinks. For all these joys
    we thank You, Lord.   Amen.

Closing

As the rain refreshes the thirsty ground, grant that what we have
heard and read and sung may refresh our spirits and cause us to grow
in You and the knowledge of Your love, Amen.

Reading

And God saw everything that he had   Genesis 1: 1–13
made, and behold, it was very good. (Gen. 1: 31)

Almighty God, Creator of all living things,
  We thank You for the joy of our gardens.
  We thank You for the miracle of life that bursts forth from the
    seeds and bulbs we plant and tend.
  We thank You for the beauty of the flowers and shrubs and trees
    that delight our eyes.
  We thank You for the satisfaction we gain from keeping the
    weeds at bay, and the lawns well mown.
  We thank You for the peace we find as we work or rest in our
    gardens.
  We thank You for the pleasure we gain from giving others the
    flowers or vegetables we have grown.
  We worship You for the colours, the shapes and the perfume of
    all growing things, and give You all our thanks.   Amen.

Lord, we would remember in our prayers those whose lives are
    concerned with growing things: the farmers who grow the
    grain for flour and bread; the market gardeners who grow
    vegetables and fruit; the men who make and keep our parks and
    public gardens so beautiful. Bless them in their work and keep
    them in health of body, mind and soul. In Your Name we ask
    it, Amen.

Closing

O God, our Father, as the plants and trees grow in our gardens,
grant too that we may grow in grace and the knowledge of Your
truth. We ask it in the Name of the Lord Jesus Christ, Amen.

FOR THOSE WHO LIVE IN TOWNS

Opening

Reading

Acts 18: 5–11

"Do not be afraid but speak, and do not
be silent; for I am with you, and no
man shall attack you to harm you; for
I have many people in this city." (Acts 18: 9, 10)

Lord, we think today of those of Your people who spend their lives
in towns and cities. We think of those whose jobs bring them
together in big factories and offices, and whose homes are in blocks
of flats or overcrowded houses, where there is little opportunity for
peace and privacy. We think of those whose ears are constantly
assailed by noise—the noise of machinery and of traffic and the
voices of their fellow-men.

Lord, in these conditions, it is difficult to hear Your voice above
the clamour of the world, and to seek Your face amongst the crowds.
Lord, make Yourself known and give men Your peace.   Amen.

Lord, grant that men and women may not be so concerned with
getting that they forget to give.
That they may not be so concerned with speaking that they
forget to listen.
That they may not be so concerned with crowds that they forget
the individual.
That they may not be so concerned with living that they forget
someday they must die.
That the knowledge that one day we must give an account of our
lives, may influence all that we say and do. In Your Name we ask
it, Amen.

Closing

Be not far from each one of us, O Lord, for in You we live and
move and have our being.   Amen.

FOR THOSE WHO LIVE BY THE SEA

Opening

Let us thank the Lord for His steadfast
love, for His wonderful works to the
sons of men. (Ps. 107: 21)

Reading

Psalm 107: 23–32

We ask Your blessing, Lord, on all those who live by the sea and
make their livelihood from it:

For fishermen and sailors and the crews of pleasure boats and ocean-going ships:	In their dealing with the dangers of the sea, protect them.
For hotel keepers and land-ladies and those who rent out caravans or camping sites:	In their dealings with other people, encourage them to be just and fair.
For coastguards and lifeguards and the pilots and captains of Air Sea rescue helicopters and launches:	In their sacrifice of self for others, uphold them.

In Your Name we ask it, Amen.

Heavenly Father, We ask that Your protection may rest upon those
who man the lifeboats along the dangerous stretches of our coasts.
We pray for the wives and mothers and sisters who see their menfolk
go out, never knowing if they will return. Bless these men for their
courage as they risk their lives for others with no thought of reward
or gain, and remind us to support them through our prayers and
gifts. Amen.

Closing

Whoever is wise gives heed to the things of the Lord and considers
His steadfast love towards us and all men. Amen.

FOR SHOP ASSISTANTS AND CUSTOMERS

Opening   *Reading*

Having gifts that differ according to   Romans 12: 6–17
the grace given to us, let us use them:
if prophecy, in proportion to our faith;
if service, in our serving. (Rom. 12: 6, 7)

Almighty God, who has given to each one of us different ability and
different capacity for service, we bring to You today all those whose
job it is to serve in shops and supermarkets. We know that they are
often tired and footsore; that they are often sorely tried by unreasonable and irritable customers; they are often bored by the
monotony of their work; they must often be discontented with long
hours and low wages.

Lord, give them fresh heart for their work and a new outlook.
Show them that all service can be noble if it is done for You and
remind those who are Your servants that You said, "He who would
be greatest among you must be the servant of you all." Amen.

Lord, help us to be the kind of customer who is a joy to serve; to
be polite, especially when we have cause to be rude; to be patient
especially when we are kept waiting for an unreasonable period; to
explain clearly what we require, and not to blame the shop assistant
if it is not available.

And as we wait in queues or stand in front of counters, remind us
to redeem the time of waiting with a prayer for the one who is
serving. In Your Name we ask it, Amen.

Closing

Let us all love one another with brotherly affection, and outdo one
another in showing honour. May we never flag in zeal, always be
aglow with the Spirit, serving the Lord. (Adapted from Rom. 12:
10–11.) Amen.

A WORKING PARTY

Opening　　　　　　　　　　　　　　　　　*Reading*

And when he (Peter) had come they took　　　Acts 9: 36–43
him to the upper room. All the widows
stood beside him weeping, and showing
coats and garments which Dorcas made
while she was with them. (Acts 9: 39)

Lord, as we gather here today to work for You through the skill of
　　　our fingers, grant that we may be conscious of Your presence
　　　with us, and Your approval upon our activities. May the
　　　garments and articles upon which we are working be seen as
　　　tokens of Your love and care, and may they be used to clothe
　　　the needy and provide funds for the continuance of Your work.
　　　May the joy of working together deepen the fellowship of our
　　　group and increase the interest and concern we have for each
　　　other. In Your Name we ask it, Amen.

Almighty God, we remember in prayer those whom we seek to
　　　support by our work: our missionary brothers and sisters who
　　　will receive the garments, and be encouraged because we have
　　　cared; the very old and the very young who will be warmed in
　　　body and spirit because we have thought about them; those
　　　who will sell what we have made so that money will be
　　　available for what is needed.
Father, the work that we are doing seems so insignificant, yet we
know we are tiny links in the great chain of Your love encircling the
world. Thank You for this knowledge and help us to be strong
links for the sake of those we serve.　Amen.

Closing

Bless, O Lord, the work we have accomplished, and accept our
thanks for the fellowship we have enjoyed, and continue to use us
in Your service, we pray You.　Amen.

VISITING

Opening   *Reading*

Religion that is pure and undefiled before   James 1: 22–27
God and the Father is this: to visit
orphans and widows in their affliction, and
to keep oneself unstained from the world. (James 1: 27)

Lord Jesus Christ, who commanded us to meet the needs of the
hungry and thirsty, to clothe the naked and to visit the sick, the
stranger and those in prison, we ask that Your compassion and
courage will fill our hearts, as we prepare to obey. Lead us to the
lonely, the sad and the sick, and show us how we can best serve
them. Prepare the way for us so that we may find them responsive.
Help us to be sensitive and tactful in all we say and do. Guide us in
our choice of gift and may it be given and received with gracious-
ness. Help us to be good listeners and sparing with advice. Show us
when we should speak of You and how to do it. Lord, as we go as
Your ambassadors, grant that we may not let You down.   Amen.

Lord, we have full and busy lives and may not know what it is like
  to sit alone, longing for a knock at the door and someone to
  talk to.
Lord, we are fit and strong and find it hard to imagine what it is like
  to be in bed day after day, suffering pain that no one wants to
  hear about.
Lord, we are young and agile. How can we understand what it is
  like to be old and helpless with eyes that are dim, ears that are
  deaf and limbs that are stiff and clumsy.
Lord, we will seek out the lonely, the sick, the old, and bring them
  into the warmth of our fellowship.   Amen.

Closing

Now may the God of peace who brought again from the dead our
Lord Jesus, the great shepherd of the sheep . . . equip you with
everything good that you may do his will, working in you that
which is pleasing in his sight, through Jesus Christ, to whom be
glory for ever and ever. (Hebrews 13: 20, 21.)   Amen.

Opening   *Reading*

After three days they found him (Jesus)   Luke 2: 41–49
in the temple, sitting among the teachers,
listening to them and asking them questions.
(Luke 2: 46)

Lord Jesus Christ, who showed to us the value of gathering together
in groups to hear and to ask questions, be with us now as we
seek to follow Your example. Give wisdom to the group
leaders, and to all of us a healthy seeking after the truth. Grant
that we do not waste time in unprofitable chatter, but restrict
our discussion to things of real and lasting value. Give us the
guidance of Your Holy Spirit and may we be prepared to
accept the authority of Your Word in all things. In Your Name
we ask it, Amen.

Loving Heavenly Father, we are gathered together today to try to
find the Christian answer to the many problems of our daily
lives.
May those who have difficulties have the courage to voice them.
May those who have been guided by You be resolved to say so.
May those who are shy of speaking be encouraged.
May those who are inclined to talk too much be restrained, so that
in sharing we may find solutions and in discussing we may be
given clear directions.
For the sake of Your Son, our Lord Jesus Christ, Amen.

Closing

Almighty God, Grant that the matters we have discussed may be of
real profit to us and that, as a result, we may live lives more worthy
of our high calling as Your servants. Amen.

FOR A BIBLE STUDY

Opening   *Reading*

Teach me, O Lord, the way of thy statutes;   Psalm 119: 9–18
and I will keep it to the end.

Give me understanding, that I may keep
thy law and observe it with my whole heart. (Ps. 119: 33, 34)

O Lord, we are gathered here today to learn from Your Word.
> Help us to fix our minds on You and take away the little
> distractions of our daily lives.
> Help us to understand things that are difficult and to apply to
> ourselves the things that are meant for us.
> Help us to store up knowledge so that we can draw upon it
> when we need it most.
> Help us to follow any leading that You may give us, to put
> aside anything that we may come to realize is bad or wrong.

Speak to us Lord, and make us ready and willing to hear and to
obey. Amen.

Almighty God, we thank You for Your Holy Word and for the
men and women who have given their lives to preserve it for
us. Teach us to value it as we should, and to read, learn and
inwardly digest its wisdom. Bless our brothers and sisters in
other lands to whom the Bible is a forbidden Book, and who
must read it in secret, and lead the Christian life in constant fear
and danger. Give them courage and Your divine protection and
the knowledge that we are upholding them with our prayers.
We ask this in the Name of the Lord Jesus. Amen.

Closing

You have dealt well with Your servants, O Lord, according to Your
Word. Teach us good judgement and knowledge for we believe in
Your commandments. Amen.

Opening   *Reading*

Wolves and sheep will live together in peace,   Genesis 1: 24-31
and leopards will lie down with young goats.
Calves and lion cubs will feed together, and
little children will take care of them. (Isaiah 11: 6-7)

O God, Who created all living creatures and gave man the dominion over them, thereby enriching our lives.

Grant that we may never be guilty of ill-treating or neglecting animals, fish or birds.

Remind us to be wary of assuming responsibilities that we may find ourselves unwilling or unable to fulfil.

Give us the courage to uncover and highlight areas where united public action can prevent cruelty and abuse.

Save us from the hypocrisy of giving lip service to animal welfare whilst withholding the time and money that can transform words into action.

Give us clear thinking over issues that concern the exploitation of dumb creatures for financial gain, so that we may be worthy of the responsibility You have placed in our hands. Amen.

Thank You, Lord, for those whose love and concern for animals has led them to devote their lives to animal welfare.

Encourage and sustain veterinary surgeons, nurses and lay assistants, who often work long and unsocial hours in difficult conditions in order to relieve animal suffering and restore good health.

Give them patience, gentleness, tact, wisdom and energy, and the determination to combat ignorance and prejudice wherever it is to be found. May they experience the satisfaction and fulfilment that is the reward of all those who are engaged in worthwhile work to which they feel called and for which they have been trained. Amen.

Closing

Dear Father God, Motivate us to take action whenever and wherever we find the creatures you created suffering from cruelty, neglect or indifference at the hands of man, woman or child, and convict us when we shy away from personal involvement. Amen.

HOSPICES

Opening   *Reading*
Even if I go through the deepest darkness   1 Cor. 12: 4–11
I will not be afraid, Lord. (Psalm 23: 4)

Lord Jesus Christ,
> We thank You for those who follow in your footsteps and dedicate their lives to the care of those who suffer in body, mind and spirit.
> We know that because of the nature of their work they must often feel weary, sad and depressed.
> We ask that you will renew, strengthen, and encourage them, and help us by our interest and the giving of time and money, to make their valuable task a little easier to perform.
> In Your Name we ask it. Amen.

Dear Father God,
> We pray for those who suffer — especially any who are personally known to us.
> For those whose bodies are diseased, broken, or worn out.
> For those who have been born with a particular disability which they have had to learn to live with for the whole of their lives.
> For those who suffer mental illness, which makes them confused, unstable, violent, frightened or childlike in their behaviour.
> For those who bring sickness upon themselves through their own weakness, and yet find it impossible to change their life-style.
> We confess that we do not wholly understand the reason for much of the world's suffering, but we do believe that You care, and our prayers do not go unheard, because we pray them in the name of Your Son, Jesus Christ, our Lord. Amen.

Closing

Bless, dear Lord, all those who have the gift of healing, relieving suffering, and speaking a message of comfort, hope and courage to those who are terminally ill. May we remember in our prayers both them and those they serve, in Jesus' name. Amen.

BIBLICAL INDEX

(R) = Reading
(O) = Opening